Social Capital and Entrepreneurship

Social Capital and Entrepreneurship

Phillip H. Kim and Howard E. Aldrich

Sociology Department,
University of North Carolina at Chapel Hill,
NC 27599-3210, USA

howard_aldrich@unc.edu

the essence of knowledge

Boston – Delft

Foundations and Trends™ in Entrepreneurship

Published, sold and distributed by:
now Publishers Inc.
PO Box 1024
Hanover, MA 02339
USA
Tel. +1-781-985-4510
www.nowpublishers.com
sales@nowpublishers.com

Outside North America:
now Publishers Inc.
PO Box 179
2600 AD Delft
The Netherlands
Tel. +31-6-51115274

A Cataloging-in-Publication record is available from the Library of Congress.

Printed on acid-free paper

ISBN:
© 2005 Phillip H. Kim and Howard E. Aldrich

Contents

1

Introduction

In 2002, Friendster launched a web-based social networking tool that allowed individuals to take advantage of the internet by actively managing their own social connections. Backed by venture capital investors from Kleiner, Perkins, Caufield & Byers and Benchmark Capital, Friendster built upon a simple idea: give users a tool to leverage their social ties so that they could reach distant others who might have similar interests. Friendster accomplished this by creating a visual representation of a user's social network and by providing capabilities for storing relevant information, thus giving users the ability to find and create ties to other users.

The creators of Friendster knew that individuals keep in touch with their strong ties on a frequent basis. However, if people rely only on their strong ties, their networking prospects are severely limited. Given time and geographic constraints, most individuals have very few strong ties, typically ranging from five to twenty relationships ([30]; [57]). In contrast, people have many weak ties, but managing these relationships is much more difficult than managing strong ties. Without frequent and reciprocated contact, people find it difficult to keep track of changes in the lives of their contacts, such as career moves or the birth of a child. Friendster made it easy to monitor such changes by automating the tie management process. Additionally, Friendster's users were able to increase their network reach by "meeting" other users through their direct ties.

Entrepreneurs have also recognized the possibilities of translating social network principles into practical and accessible solutions. Websites, books, articles, seminars, and voluntary associations have sprung up to serve the perceived networking needs of individuals wishing to start new firms or expand existing businesses. Consequently, the population of networking websites has grown rapidly since Friendster's inception in 2002. As of early 2005, there were at least 30 online networking sites (as listed by friendsurfer.com). This population was divided into two niches: social- and business-oriented networking. Ecademy, Ryze, and Open Business Club are leading sites oriented towards cultivating business and professional relationships. The website run by 5MinuteNetworking offers evening "meeting events" at which people can meet other business people.

In addition to the upsurge of online networking sites, traditional networking formats continue to thrive. For example, Gray Hair Management hosts structured networking events that enable participants to meet and exchange information with other participants. Since its establishment in 1995, the Silicon Valley Area of Startup Entrepreneurs has provided a forum for local entrepreneurs to interact with other professionals, as well as sponsoring networking events. College and professional schools sponsor local clubs to facilitate regional exchange among their alumni. Books such as *Nonstop Networking* [65] and *Achieving Success through Networking* [8] offer specific advice on how to build and maintain productive professional networks. Seminars costing several hundred dollars continue to attract interested individuals wanting to learn about developing relationship skills.

1.1. Why do people need networking help?

The growth of so many organizations and associations devoted to helping people create and maintain social networks poses a puzzle for social scientists. Why do people need any help? Social relations seem fundamental to everyone's life and would appear to follow naturally from growing up in organized social settings. Throughout their life course, people are embedded in social situations that put them in touch with others, such as kin reunions, gatherings of friends, workplace teams, and voluntary association meetings. Nonetheless, we suggest that cultivating and maintaining valuable relationships through one's social network requires skills that cannot be generated by habitual social behavior. We argue that, left to follow its natural course, everyday networking comes up against a set of significant social constraints that renders its use problematic for many entrepreneurs.

To convey a sense of the inherent constraints on social networks, we offer a simple scenario. Consider a situation in which an entrepreneur seeks resources from resource providers beyond his or her immediate set of direct ties – people known directly on a face-to-face basis. Assume that the entrepreneur ("ego") has 100 direct ties with other individuals ("alters") in his or her network. Then assume that each of the 100 alters has 100 direct ties in their networks. At this point, ego can access 10,000 additional individuals indirectly through the 100 alters with whom ego has a direct tie (i.e., $100 \times 100 = 10,000$ ties). If we assume each of the 100 first-order alters also has 100 direct ties with a second-order alter, ego can access an additional one million individuals indirectly (i.e., $100 \times 100 \times 100 = 1,000,000$ ties). Thus, by leveraging their direct ties, entrepreneurs can reach out within two steps to one million potential resource providers!

This simple example illustrates how increasing the reach of their networks can motivate users on Friendster or similar networking services to examine and sustain their personal networks. Rather than being limited to a small set of persons known directly, entrepreneurs can, in theory, gain what they need by taking advantage of the wider social network in which their direct ties are embedded. Our example illustrates why entrepreneurship researchers have responded so favorably to the concepts and principles of social network analysis and the associated concept of social capital.

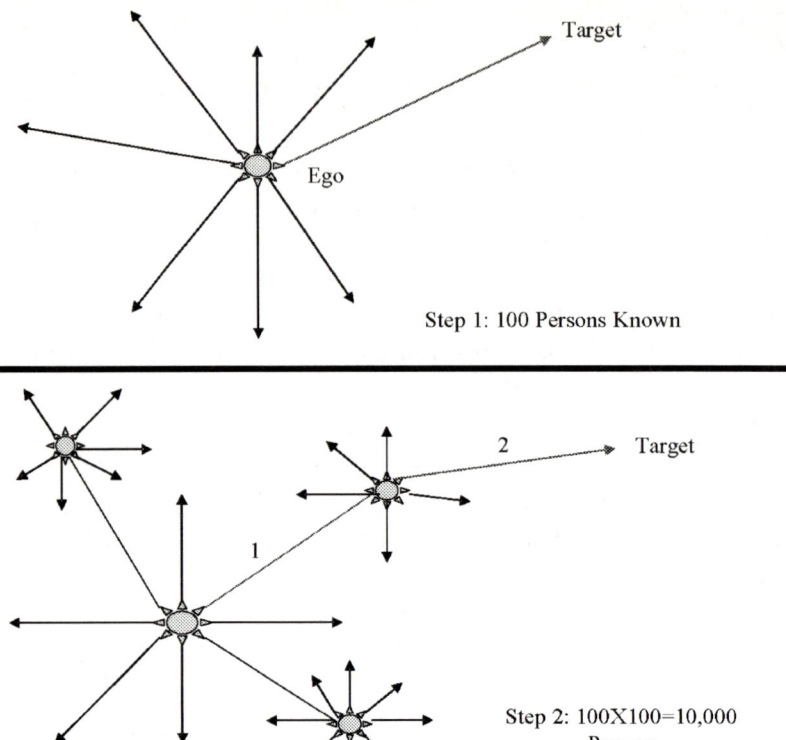

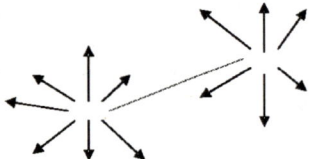

Fig. 1.1 The Potential of Indirect Ties

In this Section, we define *social capital* broadly as the resources available to people through their social connections ([20]; [53]).[1] In our

---

[1] Our aim in this Section is to highlight and apply relevant social network principles to entrepreneurship research. We acknowledge that ongoing debates surrounding the definition of *social*

example, an entrepreneur holds out the dream of an expansive playing field. With a perceived unlimited personal reach, an entrepreneur pursues their needs as they please, limited only by their ability to recognize opportunities within the social network. Using their social ties skillfully, entrepreneurs can apparently reap substantial returns on their social capital and boost their chances of commercial success. However, a comparison of this dream to social reality reveals serious flaws in its logic.

1.2. Socio-cultural constraints on social networks

We offer three explanations for why our optimistic example of an entrepreneur's network reaching almost a million people, starting from those directly known to him or her, cannot be fully realized by most individuals. First, individuals' networks often lack significant *diversity*. Instead, individuals' networks, as well as networks within associations, organizations, and communities, are often homogenous along key dimensions, such as race, age, and sex. In our example, we assumed that each first-order alter had 100 unique direct ties with second-order alters which thus created an exponential effect of increasing indirect ties. Because individuals with similar backgrounds and interests are more likely to associate with one another, rather than with people with dissimilar backgrounds, social networks are typically characterized by a lack of diversity ([11]; [62]). In the language of social networks, the friends of our friends are already our friends, rather than strangers.

Second, social boundaries create obstacles that inhibit the emergence of social relationships. Much of a person's social life is lived within the boundaries of family and kinship relations, religious and ethnic communities, language groups, and other limits to unfettered social action. Strong boundaries deflect social relationships back upon themselves, thus fostering highly concentrated social networks. Although most of these boundaries are quasi-permeable, surmounting them requires work that people are often discouraged from undertaking.

---

capital continue. Adler and Kwon [1] compiled a list of definition under three categories (external, internal and combination of both). For reviews of these debates, including alternative definitions, we refer readers to Burt [18], Fine [29], Kadushin [44], Lin [53], and Portes [70].

Interacting across social boundaries may require learning a new language and new customs, as well as tolerating a high level of ambiguity. Additionally, people's own groups often actively discourage contact with dissimilar others.

Third, because individuals lack clairvoyance and thus cannot know the full potential of pursuing indirect network ties, ignorance and uncertainty limit their activities. Ignorance and uncertainty, in turn, leave people with only *bounded rationality*, rather than hyper-rationality, in their pursuit of new relationships. The Carnegie school tradition of March and Simon [54] noted two features common to all social behavior: first, people operate within the constraints of *bounded rationality* and second, much of human behavior is driven by *opportunism*. Most people are intendedly rational but cannot achieve textbook rationality because of human cognitive deficiencies and peculiarities, limits on information availability, and constraints on information processing. Information search costs, in particular, lead most people to choose satisfactory, rather than optimal, alternatives. People must also contend with the tendency of others to behave opportunistically, self-centeredly pursuing their own self-interest. Without mechanisms for reducing uncertainty, such as endorsements or relying on brokers, individuals hesitate to initiate new relationships.[2] Entrepreneurs will forfeit potentially valuable relationships because they have no clue as to which network paths they should pursue.

Underlying all three constraints is an issue facing people whenever they go beyond relationships with people already known to them: lack of *trust*. According to theories of transaction cost economizing, people tend to lie, cheat, and steal to further their own ends [89]. They withhold information or distort it, conceal preferences, and practice a variety of other deceptions. Relationships characterized by trust between persons require an environment in which social norms can be enforced and reciprocated. Relationships that are socially embedded reduce the potential of opportunistic behavior by either person ([36]; [85]). In our

---

[2] Podolny [68] described this dilemma in terms of ego- and alter-centric uncertainty. For a relationship to form between ego and alter, both actors need to overcome substantial uncertainties. For example, an entrepreneur faces ego-centric uncertainty when evaluating potential suppliers with whom to conduct business, while a selected supplier experiences alter-centric uncertainty when evaluating the creditworthiness of a new customer (i.e., the entrepreneur).

example, reaching beyond the initial circle of 100 direct ties would expose entrepreneurs to persons about whom they know little or nothing. Going beyond their known world, facing uncertainty and social boundaries, their easiest path is to fall back upon familiar contacts. In strategic terms, entrepreneurs who find ways to get around the problem of trust, e.g. by finding substitutes for it, will have an advantage over others.

Thus, despite the great promise of earning high returns on their social capital, entrepreneurs' efforts often fall short. Even though their social ties potentially link them to dissimilar others at great remove and thus enhance their access to opportunities and resources, the constraints we have just noted make problematic purely instrumental action within networks. Instead, the embedded nature of social networks means that entrepreneurs' attempts to start and grow their organizations often come up against significant socio-cultural constraints. Understanding the association between social capital and entrepreneurship thus requires that we investigate more thoroughly the social and cultural context of entrepreneurial networking. From this inquiry, a more nuanced and thorough understanding of entrepreneurial actions emerges.

In the remainder of this text, we analyze three empirical observations about social networks, show how the concepts of homophily, social boundaries, and bounded rationality provide a framework for understanding the observations, and present examples of each from the entrepreneurship literature. We discuss three observations: (1) relationships are often based on people with similar characteristics and the resulting lack of diversity limits people's access to opportunities and resources; (2) not all relationships are valued the same way, with some bridging gaps between diverse locations and others merely serving as dead ends; and (3) some people are sought out more than others, with their centrality giving them power and prestige they use to their advantage. We also introduce relevant social network tools to study these observations.

2

Observation 1: Social networks tend toward homogeneity, not diversity

---

In Friendster, users complete a profile listing their background information, hobbies, and other notable affiliations and memberships. Based on this information, they can search for others with similar interests and backgrounds. Since people typically form relationships with others who resemble themselves, this type of routine social behavior extends to users searching for similar others using online tools. Social scientists have extensively documented the generalization that "birds of a feather flock together" since the early 20th century ([5]; [13]; [88]). Studies range from research on friendships [51] and teams [75] to studies of cultural and voluntary associations ([25]; [59]) and business organizations ([43]; [45]).

Homophily constitutes the central principle behind these consistent findings. Homophily occurs when people with similar characteristics are attracted to one another, especially within distinct social boundaries, such as language and nationality, and when the structure of the social world makes it difficult for people with dissimilar characteristics to associate with one another ([11]; [62]). The characteristics that bring individuals together can be either *ascribed* and thus not easily changed by individual choice, such as demographic background (age, ethnicity, and sex) or *achieved* and thus potentially open to change by individuals, such as education, work experience, and occupation. In practice, relationships form through combinations of ascribed and achieved characteristics.

Limitations on information collection and interpretation restrict an individual's knowledge of the world, making associations with dissimilar others difficult to occur. Restrictions on associative activities create a recursive cycle – given knowledge constraints, individuals become habituated to seeking out similar others and uncomfortable with dissimilar others [60]. Overcoming this tendency requires that individuals either pro-actively make strategic choices that push them across social boundaries or become involved in activities that unintentionally expose them to dissimilar others. However, individuals who pursue this strategy are likely to have less stable relationships and will need to bear the additional costs generated by bridging differences ([6]; [69]). For example, in her ethnographic research in Silicon Valley, English-Lueck [26] heard stories of Indian workers researching American political jokes to facilitate small talk with their American colleagues and thus ease working relationships.

2.1. Relational homogeneity and diversity in entrepreneurial networks: two concepts

In applying the concept of homophily to entrepreneurship and social capital, we highlight two social network concepts that draw on the concept of relational diversity: small world networks and affiliation networks. We summarize these concepts in Table 2.1.

2.1.1. Small world networks

Two important characteristics define the small world network concept: first, *local networks* in which relationships cluster together and second, *bridging ties* that join local networks together to form a global network [87]. Beginning with Milgram's [63] study of the ties linking a random sample of people in Omaha, Nebraska to a Sharon, Massachusetts stockbroker, social scientists have argued that even individuals who

Small world networks	Affiliation networks
• Particularistic recruiting principles • Lower turnover among similar others • Homophily as a screening mechanism • Network closure and density	• Two mode networks (actor x affiliation) • Multiple affiliations lead to greater diversity and reinforce existing relationships • However, difficulties in sustaining multiple memberships

Table 2.1 Homogeneity in Relationships – Summary

appear to have a constricted set of relationships can actually be connected to socially and geographically distant individuals. In this Section, we focus on the formation of local networks and then elaborate on the role of bridging ties to distant individuals in the following Section.

Particularistic rather than universalistic principles govern the way in which in which most people become members of local networks. Instead of extending an open public invitation to join, existing clusters recruit new members either by specifically recruiting them (e.g., Friendster users send an invitation via email to other potential users) or through drawing on their current ties in other domains (e.g., through kinship ties). Because individuals who share similar characteristics are more likely to know each other, these individuals tend to form dense clusters in which everyone knows everyone else. For example, in Friendster, an individual forms an interest group by creating linkages with other individuals having similar interests, thus creating a local network of individuals who know each other through their shared circumstances.

In developing relationships with others, propinquity and the logistical difficulty of finding physically distant individuals also constrain members in local networks [11]. For example, individuals in densely populated urban areas will have greater opportunities to form multiple local networks based on distinct common interests than individuals in rural areas. Friendster and other automated networking technologies were developed, in part, to overcome propinquity constraints, such as geography.

Dense local networks can lead to three self-reinforcing dynamics that reproduce and exaggerate their tendency toward narrow clustering.

First, new actors wishing to join an existing local network face potential barriers when they do not share common experiences and interests with current members. For example, kin-based network clusters may squeeze out non-kin who would otherwise benefit from membership [57]. In their study of entrepreneurs in the Research Triangle area, Renzulli, Aldrich, and Moody [73] found having a higher proportion of kin in their network reduced the likelihood of people starting a new business.

Second, similarities among individuals create stronger linkages and reduce the likelihood of turnover within a local network. Conversely, dissimilarities increase the likelihood of people leaving relationships. For example, Popielarz and McPherson [69] reported the likelihood of leaving voluntary associations increased as differences between a member's educational attainment and the average educational attainment for an organization increased.

Third, if homophily serves as a basis for recruiting similar others, this common characteristic could be used as a screening mechanism. In their work on hiring practices at a phone center, Fernandez, Castilla, and Moore [28] reported that new hires referred by current employees were more likely to be similar to current employees than non-referred new hires.[1] These three self-reinforcing dynamics, built on homophily and propinquity, alter the configuration of local networks.

In turn, local networks, formed and sustained by these three dynamics, affect entrepreneurs in two ways. First, according to Coleman [20], network closure constitutes a primary source of social capital. Within closed networks, social norms are monitored and enforced more easily. In a dense network, violators suffer the consequences of local sanctioning, such as loss of reputation, when they violate norms. Within closed networks, violators will confront a "united front" composed of fellow actors who call for a remedy. For example, rotating credit associations rely on collective trust among their members and take advantage of the benefits of network closure [10]. At the credit association's inception, members decide how much they will contribute during each period and choose a method for determining how the money will be awarded at the end of each period. If the level of trust and the

---

[1] They argued these results showed that current employees know what type of person would be more likely to succeed at the firm and thus could make a more effective referral.

efficacy of the monitoring system are sufficient, members stay in the association until all have been paid off, rather than defecting as soon as their own turn has paid off.

Second, the high density of a small world network can have positive or negative consequences for entrepreneurs. *Density* refers to the extent to which alters in an individual's network know one another. High-density networks can be useful because they provide social support and facilitate the transmission of complicated information ([64]; [67]). Some research has also claimed that high-density networks can foster economic relations through the creation of trust. High-density networks, however, can also be detrimental to the extent that they induce conformity and constrain individuals' autonomy, creativity, and innovation ([14]; [17]; [33]; [35]; [39]; [71]). When networks are dense, the potential assistance available from different members is often redundant because information and potential contacts are likely to be widely shared [34]. Additional network members in a dense network fail to provide novel information and resources.

For example, by using online networking tools such as Friendster, an individual can theoretically develop relationships throughout a global network of users. However, without relying on external support mechanisms, most are unable to see beyond their local networks. The "6 degrees from Kevin Bacon" and other variations of this cocktail game are empirically valid – people *can* be connected with many others within 4 to 6 degrees. Nevertheless, individuals do not often form relationships that link their local networks with distant others who themselves are members of local networks [87].

2.1.2. Affiliation networks

Social network researchers refer to actors' multiple memberships in different types of organized social entities as *affiliation networks* [15]. If we have information on an actor n's affiliations with different entities (e.g. m organizational membership), we can use this information to construct a two mode network. For a two-mode affiliation matrix $\mathbf{A}$, using matrix algebra, we could build an (n by n) actor by actor matrix by post-multiplying $\mathbf{A}$ with its transpose ($\mathbf{AA'}$) and an (m by m) organization by organization matrix by pre-multiplying $\mathbf{A}$ with its transpose $(\mathbf{A'A})$. Such datasets and analyses can reveal the extent to which actors are affiliated with certain types of organizations. For example, Galaskiewicz [32] collected data on 26 CEOs in the Minneapolis/St. Paul region and their board memberships in 15 organizations. Cornwell and Harrison [21] used this logic to explain unions' relative lack of political impact in the United States in the late 20th century. They showed that the relative lack of participation by union members in other types of voluntary associations limited their contact with non-union members and constrained their ability to influence non-members' political beliefs.

When applied to entrepreneurs, the analysis of affiliation networks allows us to explore whether some configurations of networks are more likely to facilitate access to opportunities and resources than others. For example, Davis, Renzulli, and Aldrich [22] showed that, under certain conditions, active participation in a range of different voluntary organizations increased occupational diversity among their business discussion networks. Simply belonging to multiple associations had no affect on owners' networks. Owners benefited from association membership only when they belonged to multiple associations and met their discussion partners in different associations. Owners whose discussion partners were concentrated in a small number of associations had high-density and low-diversity networks, which Renzulli, Aldrich, and Moody [73] showed lowered the likelihood of additional business startups.

Affiliation networks can also be used to study connections between organizations produced by joint memberships. Entrepreneurs can benefit from two potential scenarios. First, entrepreneurs with memberships in multiple organizations with few connections between them could benefit because the total potential number of new relationships could increase. However, in practice, entrepreneurs will encounter difficulties when sustaining multiple memberships, because entrepreneurs need to bridge several local networks simultaneously. The competition among organizations for a member's sustained commitment eventually increases the likelihood of membership turnover among highly sought-after members [69]. Nonetheless, entrepreneurs who are able to sustain multiple memberships in non-overlapping organizations should gain more rapid access to diverse information and opportunities than entrepreneurs moving in more constricted circles.

Second, when organizational connections are dense, members' multiple shared memberships in other organizations reinforce relationships that exist within the local network of a single organization. For example, Useem [84] described how board of director members in large American and British corporations had multiple memberships in exclusive metropolitan business clubs. Within the context of these club memberships, reputations are established, knowledge is shared, and business opportunities are identified. With regard to the diffusion of new business practices through networks, many studies show both rapid and slow movement through such networks. For example, corporate board interlocks in the 1970s and 80s strongly affected the spread of the "poison-pill" takeover [23].

The "poison-pill" defense against being taken over by outside firms spread rapidly through ties between corporate boards, with firms adopting the practice to the extent that their trusted contacts had done so. Ties between corporate board members raised the visibility of the practice and made it legitimate. By contrast, "golden parachutes" for departing executives spread slowly, with little evidence that directors' contacts through corporate boards made any difference. Despite ties to others who adopted it, the corporate elite looked at it ambivalently, because golden parachutes appeared as naked self-interest on the part of management. Entrepreneurs within densely connected networks thus become susceptible to fads and fashions, with the wider cultural context affecting their degree of susceptibility [81].

In affiliation networks, members need to meet a set of formalized entry criteria before being admitted to valued organizations. Often, whether stated explicitly or not, these criteria include ascribed and achieved characteristics on which homophilous relationships are based. In their historical studies, Baltzell [9] and Domhoff [24] described how "high society" clubs have used characteristics such as gender, race, cultural heritage, wealth, and religion to qualify certain members. Excluded groups have also mobilized and formed associations to cater to a specific demographic background, such as the Committee of 200, National Association of Women Business Owners, and Asian Women in Business. Prospective students make considerable financial investments to enroll in respected professional schools in order to participate in alumni networks and benefit from introductions due simply to their common educational affiliation. Whether membership scope is local (i.e., Triangle area alumni club) or national, recruitment based on homophily allows relatively few to qualify.

Entrepreneurs can maximize opportunities for identifying new business prospects and information by adopting a portfolio of multiple, non-overlapping memberships in various associations and organizations [22]. However, entrepreneurs face obstacles in assembling an optimal, diverse membership portfolio. These barriers include qualifying for membership in alternative organizations and, if qualified, accessibility to these organizations, given time and location constraints.

2.2. Summary

In a locally dense network, over time, entrepreneurs will face limited access to new resources and knowledge if local networks are not connected to other local networks [19]. Within local networks, people share the same pool of knowledge and feel comfortable together because of their similar backgrounds and interests. The resulting network closure creates benefits for members, such as trust development, meticulous enforcement of norms, and rapid diffusion of knowledge. If entrepreneurs develop ties with other local networks, such as those in voluntary associations, they may retain these benefits over the long-term. Our analysis implies that the benefits fall mainly to entrepreneurs able to develop a broader, more diverse network. Otherwise, faced with bounded rationality, individuals tend to rely on the safety of familiarity and remain in homogeneous relationships, rather than pursue potential gains from a more diverse network.

3

Observation 2: Not all relationships are the same

When users in Friendster enroll and begin to form their online network, they also invite their friends to join. Although we tend to ignore solicitations from unknown individuals, we usually take seriously invitations from individuals we know. Indeed, we usually respond quickly to inquiries from our closest friends. Because they take advantage of the trust that characterizes close relationships, relationship marketing strategies exploit such tendencies very effectively.

It might seem that relying upon people well known to us would be the most secure and effective way to get the information and resources we need. Family members, close friends, work colleagues, and others with whom we're well acquainted constitute our most trusted social relations. However, network analysts have pointed out two difficulties people face in building and maintaining such ties. First, sustaining strong, intensive, and trustworthy relations requires heavy investments of time and resources, and so most peoples' social relationships never become strong. Instead, social networks tend to be composed of a mix of variable strength ties. Second, the set of persons known to us directly represents only a small fraction of all the possible valuable relations we might wish to draw on. As we noted earlier, lack of diversity, semi-permeable social boundaries, and lack of clairvoyance substantially limit the value of most peoples' direct ties. Instead, the true value of networks and their associated social capital arises from individuals' abilities to make use of *indirect* ties.

Thus, in this Section, we focus on the causes and consequences of variation in the strength of social relations. We note various analytic tools that theorists have offered for differentiating "strong" from "weak" ties and the entrepreneurial implications of variations in tie strength. We note that even though investigators have spent a great deal of time examining the strength of *direct* ties, the real significance of social networks lies in the role *indirect* ties play in giving people access to social capital. We thus conclude this Section with an analysis of structural holes and the role of brokers in entrepreneurship. We summarize this Section in Table 3.1.

3.1. Variations in the strength of social ties

Tie strength varies widely across an individual's portfolio of relationships. Referring to an earlier example, a person may have 100 direct ties with other alters in his or her network, and tie strength will vary across this set. Because the level and mode of investment required to maintain relationships differs from person to person, some relationships will be stronger than others. Geographic proximity will also affect relationship maintenance. Although technological improvements such as wireless connectivity reduce geographic barriers to spending time with others, conveying sensitive information and calling someone to account are still best done during face to face interactions.

3.1.1. Dimensions of tie strength

Theoretically, tie strength is a continuous measure, ranging from having no relationship (two actors are strangers) through passing acquaintance to having a strong relationship. In turn, tie strength can be broken down into four dimensions: time spent in the relationship; its emotional intensity; the extent of mutual confiding of information; and the degree of reciprocity between the two individuals [37]. Investigators can measure these four dimensions of tie strength and then aggregate them

Tie strength	Indirect ties
• Measurement approaches • Triadic closure • Multiplexity	• Structural holes and sparse networks • Bridging and brokering scenarios • Measurement issues: ego vs full network data

Table 3.1 Variations in Relationships – Summary

to form a composite score. For example, Marsden and Campbell [58] developed a measurement model based on three of the four dimensions (data on reciprocity were not available) and tested their model on data from three separate regional studies. Their results indicated that emotional intensity appeared to be the best indicator of tie strength. In practice, due to difficulties in measurement and data collection, researchers do not obtain information on all four dimensions of tie strength. Instead, researchers most often rely on frequency of contact and emotional intensity as indicators of tie strength (e.g., Hurlbert, Haines, and Beggs [42]).

As a further analytical simplification, researchers typically collapse tie strength into two categories: strong and weak. *Name generator* questions based on the emotional intensity of a tie are used to identify strong ties, such as in the General Social Survey [57] and in studies of large corporations [16]. These survey questions are designed to solicit from respondents the names of up to five individuals with whom they engage in situations potentially laden with emotion. Topics include discussing important matters, such as political or racial issues, spending time in leisure activities, or providing career development advice [4]. Because the name generator approach is designed to identify strong ties, some investigators use the *position generator* method to capture a wider range of tie strengths.

The position generator method asks respondents whether they know people in various categories, such as public official, banker, and school teacher [53]. If respondents answer that they know someone in that category, they are then asked for details on the relationship in much the same way as in the name generator questions. Position generator questions allow investigators to discover a respondent's full range of ties and reveal gaps in relationship types that the name generator approach cannot show. For example, it can be used to show whether contact with high status positions varies systematically by social class or ethnicity.

A somewhat different approach to operationalizing tie strength is based on socio-demographic distances [11]. If similar people are more likely to associate, based on principles of homophily, these individuals are more likely than dissimilar individuals to exhibit high degrees of tie strength on each of the four dimensions [62]. For example, interracial friendships are uncommon due to low racial diversity among strong ties. Individuals with similar educational backgrounds also form strong ties [57]. Mark [55] argued that people with similar hobbies or interests not only tend to associate with one another, but also must invest heavily in sustaining these interests. They, they will have little time to develop and foster relationships with individuals having other interests.

One concept that remains understudied is that of *valence* among network relationships. Analytically, tie strength begins with a value of zero to represent no relationship between two actors and increases in value as a relationship increases in strength. Tie strength could also proceed in a negative direction – an increasingly negative value denotes stronger competition, animosity, or other attributes of relations between two actors (individuals or organizations).

Because developing a relationship along the four dimensions we have identified requires significant investments of time and resources, most individuals have few strong ties within their personal network. In his study of urban life, Fischer [30] described individuals having five to twenty strong ties. In the General Social Survey, respondents reported an average of three individuals they considered to be strong ties [57]. Limits on the distribution of strong ties are evident among entrepreneurial founding teams. Given the high level of mutual commitment and reciprocity necessary to work together on a new business venture, founding team size is small and follows a Poisson distribution [75].

3.1.2. Tie strength within groups

Researchers can identify cohesive subgroups within a network based on relationship strength principles. Nodes in a subgroups are typically linked together based, one of the following characteristics: mutuality of ties, closeness of actors, frequency of ties, and relative frequency of ties among members compared to non-members [86]. An extension of the strong tie thesis to social network analysis is the concept of triadic closure [37]. By definition, if A knows B well and B knows C well, over time A will develop a relationship with C (which could become strong). Triadic closure builds on Homans' [40] statement on the transitive nature of friendships. Subgroups may form out of triadic closure and grow in size over time.

In scenarios where triadic or network closure exists, actors develop high levels of trust among themselves. All relationships are direct, thus improving communication and knowledge transfer. Direct ties create an environment where social norms can be established and violations from these norms can be enforced through collective sanctioning, as Coleman [20] noted. One example of network closure occurs within family-run businesses. Nascent entrepreneurs often share ownership with other family members [75] and rely on them as sources of advice and support in the start-up process [46]. Family members are an initial source of reliable labor, especially in immigrant businesses (Aldrich and Waldinger, 1990), where younger generations can learn from their experienced elders [41]. Reinforced by cultural norms, business owners can rely on their kinship networks for assistance, as noted in a study of how the property rights of private entrepreneurs were enforced in China [66].

What remains unclear is a question of causal direction: does homogeneity lead to forming cohesive subgroups through more frequent contact and stronger relationships or do differences fade within relationships characterized by frequent and reciprocated contact. Friedkin [31] argued that social cohesion and greater homogeneity results from frequent contact between individuals. Because members of a subgroup are likely to access the same body of knowledge, over time, any initial advantages of differential access will eventually decline (i.e., the gossip is not news anymore) [19].

3.1.3. Multiplexity in relationships

Multiplexity refers to multiple threads or bases on which relations form between two or more people [12]. Network analysts often ignore multiple bases of relationships when they simplify relationships among actors to one type of relationship per dyadic pair. More realistically, individuals can sustain various types of relationships at different levels with the same individuals. For example, a colleague from work could also be teammate on a local softball league. Both individuals can also be neighbors and live on the same block.

We need additional studies involving the multiplexity of ties, especially to examine how relationships within different contexts affect outcomes. Can an entrepreneur cultivate a stronger relationship with a potential investor by increasing the frequency of contact through multiple types of contacts? Do social norms and expectations in one type of relationship context carry over to a separate context? For example, if a relationship is hierarchical in a family context (e.g., parent–child relations), will this role expectation impede collaboration under different conditions (e.g., parent as employee of child)? From a network analysis perspective, rather than combining multiple relationships into a single index, researchers should separate each type of relationships. Similar techniques (e.g., distance measures, blockmodeling) can be employed for each type of network relationship with results from each network relationship compared for any notable findings [86].

3.2. The power of social networks lies in indirect ties

When asked to explain the benefits of Friendster in an interview, founder Jonathan Abrams argued that the core benefit of his networking service inhered in people's ability to reach 2nd and 3rd degree relationships in their networks [74]. Once Friendster users set up their personal networks, they can preview the networks of their friends. The collective value of Friendster increases as new friends accept invitations to join and enter their own personal network online. By requesting a referral through their direct ties, people can communicate with a 2nd degree tie. By doing so, their potential for reaching additional indirect ties increases. Adding indirect ties to the mix reveals the true leveraging potential of networks and social capital.

We have noted that most people can feasibly manage only a small number of strong direct ties and thus even though they may provide security and support, reliance on them alone limits someone's networking potential. We have also noted that people can manage many more weak direct ties, but because they are less reliable, they constitute a shaky basis on which to build one's networking strategy. Indirect ties, by definition, begin as ties between strangers, as neither party knows the other directly. By taking advantage of the 2nd degree ties of their strong direct ties, entrepreneurs can build on a trusted base and gain an initial advantage for entering relationships with strangers. However, because they are not clairvoyant, entrepreneurs have only a vague picture of what lies beyond their direct ties in the larger network within which they are embedded.

3.2.1. Structural holes

Partially blind to what lies beyond their direct ties, entrepreneurs find themselves in a world of structural holes [16]. Such holes arise when networks of weaker, indirect relationships complement dense local networks of strong, direct ties. From this perspective, an analyst's emphasis shifts away from the inherent value of an entrepreneur's direct ties and towards the significance of indirect ties. This shift requires thinking more broadly about how people use network ties to reach distant relations. For example, consider a situation in which Actor A knows Actors B, C, and D and discusses business matters with each person separately on a regular basis, but B, C, and D do not know each other. Each actor maintains a personal network that does not overlap with the others'. In this scenario, structural holes separate the personal networks of Actor A's direct ties.

From a mathematical point of view, networks filled with structural holes contain few overlapping relationships between members and represent an efficient configuration for linking many actors with few ties. Entrepreneurs can exploit such network configurations in three ways: using direct ties to reach indirect ties, playing a broker's role between direct ties, and using the prestige or legitimacy of direct ties to enhance their standing with indirect ties. In the following Section, we explain each method and give examples.

First, entrepreneurs may use a direct tie to gain access to additional indirect ties. Spanning structural holes using bridging ties may join multiple small world local networks ([37]; [87]). In our earlier illustration, we posited an exponential increase in the number of indirect ties produced by successive steps outward from the focal actor. To obtain this result, we assumed a completely efficient network where each direct tie leads to *new* indirect ties.

Second, entrepreneurs can take advantage of brokering opportunities to join previous disconnected actors together, such as buyers and sellers. This brokering scenario builds on Knight's [48] definition of entrepreneurship, wherein an entrepreneur derives profits by bringing parties together, creating a market for economic exchange, and assuming the risk of a failed transaction. From this perspective, entrepreneurs need to cultivate a broad range of relationships to maintain high network efficiency and limited overlapping relationships. If successful, entrepreneurs holding this network position can become linking-pins, integrating previously disconnected local networks [3]. Linking-pin individuals or organizations can fulfill three functions: communicating information, transferring resources or clients, and serving as role models. We return to the topic of entrepreneurial brokering when we discussion our third observation, concerning centrality and prestige in social networks, in the final Section of our paper.

Third, entrepreneurs can use direct ties to provide endorsements that establish their legitimacy in the eyes of more distant network actors. Building on trust and familiarity, a direct tie can assure other indirect ties of ego's reliability, such as those typified in the relationship-marketing strategies used to grow online networks in Friendster. Entrepreneurs can play a similar by providing endorsements between different local networks (i.e., one direct tie of ego would like to meet another direct tie of ego).

The advantages of bridging and brokering indirect ties, however, are strongest in the short term [2]. When previously unconnected alters become acquainted through their strong tie relationships with ego [37], they may form direct ties with one another. Once ego strongly links disconnected actors, they no longer need ego to serve as a broker. Similarly, once credibility is established, entrepreneurs can work directly with an indirect tie without an endorsement by intermediaries.

3.2.2. The social capital researcher's dilemma

For decades, network researchers have theorized about direct and indirect ties and have shown the tremendous advantages that follow from actors' wise use of indirect ties [12]. When the concept of structural holes was introduced, entrepreneurship and strategy researchers immediately grasped its significance. Subsequently, however, an enormous gap opened between theorizing about the potential of social networks and the reality of data collection strategies based on surveying individuals. When network researchers focused mainly on villages and organizations, data collection was not problematic. However, when researchers ventured outside these relatively closed entities to study actors in more open surroundings, problems arose.

To take full advantage of the powerful analytical tools available for understanding indirect ties, researchers need network information from all the actors within a bounded entity. Using a theoretical rationale to choose an entity's boundaries allows researchers to simplify network data collection. To compile full network data at the organizational level, researchers have defined network boundaries in terms of a particular organizational population (e.g., biotechnology) or geographic location (e.g., Research Triangle Park). From these data, analysts can construct organization-sets and action-sets and use them to understand inter-organizational relationships [3].

Although entrepreneurship network analysis at an organizational level may be appealing because of the relative ease of data collection, testing social capital theories of entrepreneurship within organizations would be somewhat misleading. Because most social network theories have been developed with individual relationships in mind, researchers require full network data at the individual level. To accomplish this, they typically study a single organization, with a significant employee base working in multiple locations and divisions (e.g., Burt [16]) or pursue ethnographic research studying a limited set of research locations (e.g., Stewart [79]). With this single case approach, researchers develop theory and emphasize empirical findings.

When researchers try to transfer their single-organization or case-based models to an entrepreneurial context, they encounter many problems. They face difficulties in trying to obtain a random sample of entrepreneurs from a community or inter-organizational field, because limited time and resources constrain researchers from obtaining full network information. Time constraints limit how much information a respondent can provide, and survey costs preclude speaking to all members of a network to obtain background information.

Despite these data collection difficulties, researchers have developed several promising network concepts and tools to explore how entrepreneurs use indirect ties to complement their direct ties. For example, by using graph theoretic concepts, researchers can describe different aspects of entrepreneurs' personal networks beyond their immediate relationships [86]. To assess how accessible an entrepreneur is to various members (e.g., resource providers) in a personal network, analysts calculate several distance measures.

Based on the principle of homophily, distances among similar individuals in a network are likely to be shorter because the likelihood of interaction increases. In socio-demographic space, similar individuals will be located in the same niche and be directly tied with ego [61]. Distance between two nodes in a network can be calculated using the length of a walk, trail, or path. These three distance measures differ in terms of double counting edges or nodes (i.e., path distance is most restrictive, while walk distance is least restrictive). Geodesic distance is the shortest path if multiple pathways exist between two nodes. The diameter of the graph is largest geodesic distance in the network. Analyzing these distance measures for the entire network provides information on how reachable actors are to one another.

3.3. Summary

All social ties are not the same. Ties vary in their strength and length, affecting how resources and information flow between individuals. In trustworthy relationships, marked by frequent interactions, emotional investment, or reciprocity, both parties enjoy opportunities to discuss business matters and exchange relevant information. Future interactions that build on these interactions may be more emotionally intense or involve higher degrees of reciprocity. Entrepreneurs can count on reliable knowledge or expect promised resources. When entrepreneurs have numerous outstanding obligations, these obligations can be "called in" and counted on to comply with their requests [20]. Similarly, the other parties can provide information in confidence and expect reciprocity in the future.

As individuals become more distant from a focal entrepreneur, these relationships are less likely to be considered trustworthy. Lessened trust is offset, however, by their value via access to new information or resources. Because stronger ties lead to overlapping knowledge over time, successful entrepreneurs can avoid network closure by cultivating and maintaining indirect and weak ties. From a strategic viewpoint, entrepreneurs should form a hybrid portfolio of ties varying in strength ([7]; [85]). This portfolio can be divided into a dense local network of strong ties linked to weaker, indirect ties in the global network [72].

4

Observation 3: Some people are sought out more than others

Users of Friendster can only see networks of individuals for whom permission has been granted, either through personal invitation or through their user settings. Someone who had the ability to scan the entire Friendster network, such as a systems administrator, would see that some users stand out as more centrally active than others. These central users might have invited more individuals to join or possess certain characteristics that appeal to a wider audience. Additionally, current friends may have posted supportive testimonials, presenting a positive image and raising their profile for potential users.

For researchers studying entrepreneurship and social capital, identifying these central actors is important for at least five reasons. First, centrally located actors occupy positions which give them many advantages over less central actors. They can "see" more of the network and spot potential opportunities before others. Second, they sit astride many paths that connect people with complementary information and resources, and can act as brokers in bringing such people together. Third, their central position enables them to mobilize collective action quickly and efficiently, such as forming entrepreneurial teams, investment syndicates, and other collective commercial activities. Fourth, central actors can treat some actors preferentially by granting them access to information and resources over other actors, such as competitors. Fifth, over-reliance on a central actor creates potential vulnerabilities for peripheral actors, unless they can create additional ties to other actors.

Despite the substantive significance of central positions to people within networks, identifying them is difficult. First, very few people methodically analyze their entire personal network, taking into account their weaker direct and distant indirect ties. Lacking clairvoyance, people will inevitably concentrate their investigations on their immediate circle of friends. Indeed, they might not be able to see much beyond their direct ties. Second, without relying on a networking tool that can assemble global relationship information in an accessible manner, any inferences about the value of new ties will depend heavily on personal intuition (e.g., she seems quite popular on the lecture circuit). By contrast, independent researchers, unlike network participants, have a number of tools available to them and can therefore rise above participants' lack of clairvoyance and purely intuitive network readings.

In the remainder of this Section, we build on earlier discussions to develop our third major observation: in a global network, some actors are more central than others. Viewed from a network participant's perspective, an inherent tension exists between their difficulty in determining the actual value of network positions and their desire to improve upon them. To the extent they are unable to discern their position, their actions are blind. Nonetheless, they may intuitively grasp the value of certain strategic actions and try to increase their centrality. Regardless of their level of understanding or intentionality, entrepreneurs' actions occur within severe constraints imposed by network configurations affecting actors' centrality, directional ties, and prestige. Table 4.1 provides a summary of this Section.

4.1. Centrality measures

We note that any type of network analysis, by either a well-trained analyst or an intuitive entrepreneur, occurs within a defined context. Often, a bounded entity frames the analysis, such as an organization,

Non-directional measures	Directional measures
• Degree centrality	• Degree prestige
• Closeness centrality	• Influence domain
• Betweenness centrality	• Proximity prestige
• Information centrality	• Rank prestige

Table 4.1 Centrality in Network Relationships – Summary

village, or familial unit, populated with actors whose membership in the bounded entity qualifies them for analysis. For our example of a bounded entity within which to discuss network centrality, we use the example of an Italian garment district described by Lazerson and Lorenzoni [52]. The textile district of Prato, located near Florence, contained approximately 9,000 textile firms that employed 42,000 employees in 1997. Although Lazerson and Lorenzoni did not employ network methodologies in their study, their description implicitly referred to network concepts. We use their case study to discuss how analysts could use centrality measures to understand entrepreneurial actions and inter-organizational dynamics within a bounded space.

Urban and regional economists and geographers, as well as sociologists and historians, have emphasized the importance of conceptualizing social action as occurring within defined spatial locations [83]. Studies that identify a bounded region allow investigators to explicitly model how geographic proximity affects entrepreneurial activities, such as business foundings [77]. They also give network researchers the guidance they need to choose the persons and organizations whose relationships they wish to map. Studies of the industrial revolution in England pointed to the region-specific nature of industrial development, such as the Lancashire cotton district, and research in Europe has highlighted the importance of political and community differences across regions [78]. In the late 20th century, Silicon Valley's emergence as an icon for effective regional economic development spawned many imitators, e.g. Silicon Alley (NY) and Silicon Glen (Central Scotland). Studies such as Saxenian's [76] comparative study of Silicon Valley and the Route 129 region of New England made salient the need to study economic action within its local context.

Using global network information from a bounded entity, network analysts can measure the *centrality* of individual actors and an entire network in four different ways [86]: by degree, closeness, betweenness, and information centrality. Just as most network concepts can be studied at multiple levels of analysis, so too can centrality be defined at multiple levels. For example, we can study the centrality of individuals within organizations by examining how many people chose them and are chosen by them, and we can study centrality within an organizational population by examining which organizations receive the most choices and chose others the most.

Each centrality measure thus applies to both actor and global network levels. In our examples from Prato, we use firms rather than individuals as units of analysis.

4.1.1. Degree centrality

First, for individual actors, *degree centrality* denotes the number of direct ties associated with an actor. Actors with high degree centrality occupy positions from which they can spot new entrepreneurial opportunities, obtain new information, or serve as advisors to others. At the level of the entire network, calculating the variance of individual actors' degree centrality scores conveys a sense of whether a few actors dominate the network or ties are more equally distributed. In the Prato district, researchers could use degree centrality to identify dominant firms, based on their number of sub-contracting relationships. Using the degree centrality measures, an analyst could confirm whether most firms in the districts had sub-contracting relationships with a small number of larger firms. If so, then startups would need to build enduring relationships with the centrally active firms in order to generate revenue. If not, then new firms would enter the economic environment on an unbiased competitive footing.

4.1.2. Closeness centrality

Second, using *closeness centrality* measures, researchers can identify the *reachability* of other actors in a network to a particular actor n. Imagine a star network configuration, where ego maintains ties with five other alters, but each alter has no relations with other alters. Because each alter can access ego directly, ego exhibits high closeness centrality. Although other variations exist, a basic closeness centrality measure is an index (ranging from 0 to 1) based on the inverse of the sum of geodesic distances of relations between actor n and all other actors in the network. At the group level, closeness centrality is the variance around the mean of all actors' closeness centrality scores. High variance in the closeness centrality score at the network level indicates that a few actors are more accessible (shorter geodesics) or less accessible (greater geodesics) relative to other actors.

In the Prato district, if most small firms have a small number of significant subcontracting relationships with larger mills, star network configurations may dominate, resulting in high closeness centrality for the large mills. If subcontracting work can only be generated directly through large mills, a new textile firm would need to establish direct ties with them. Low variance in the district closeness centrality score would indicate that new firms could not rely on introductions by existing subcontractors to large mills. Closeness centrality might also be high because large mills wish to ensure timely delivery and thus avoid contractual relationships of greater than one degree, so that work does not pass through multiple subcontractors.

4.1.3. Betweenness centrality

Third, *betweenness centrality*, based on the probability that a geodesic path between two actors passes through actor n, indicates how critical an actor is along a chain of relationships. Returning to the star network configuration example, ego has high betweenness centrality because each alter must pass through ego in order to reach other alters. Actors with high betweenness centrality can act as brokers and take advantage of their central position. In the Prato District, the Best Group had high betweenness centrality and was able to compel its subcontractors to switch to new fabrics when demand lessened for its traditional woolen products. At the level of the entire network, betweenness centrality is measured as the difference between the largest actor's betweenness centrality value and actor n's betweenness centrality value.

4.1.4. Information centrality

Fourth, an *information centrality* measure is similar to betweenness centrality measures, but integrates the likelihood that actors with higher degree centrality are also more likely to be on geodesic paths between individuals. The large mills in Prato not only buy in the district but also buy and sell fabric with firms outside the district. To the extent that specialty firms rely on their partner mill to conduct business with external businesses, betweenness centrality will increase for the larger mills. Similarly, given the high level of degree centrality of the large mills, these firms will also be positioned along geodesic paths between specialty firms and textile businesses outside the Prato district.

4.2. Directional ties

Up to now, we have not distinguished any type of gradient or direction in a relationship between actors. By introducing the dimension of direction, we can explore four research questions that emerge based on directed tie information: who initiates ties, are ties reciprocated, what is the content of ties, and finally, how valuable are they?

4.2.1. Collecting longitudinal data

If they can collect longitudinal data, investigators can determine which actors initiate relationships and what conditions stimulated them. Theories of strategic entrepreneurial action sometimes posit a first-mover advantage, arguing that firms first to the market with a new product or service can establish expectations, lock in customers, and corner scarce resources. Other models suggest benefits to waiting until market conditions settle and standards have been agreed upon. Collecting data on the relative fraction of ties initiated by network actors may give researchers clues as to their relative influence. Unfortunately, many studies still rely on cross-sectional data and so directionality is often difficult to ascertain.

4.2.2. Reciprocity of ties

Knowing the direction of ties can help analysts determine if relationships are reciprocal. As a dimension of tie strength, reciprocity should be higher in strong ties. Using a data collection strategy based on cognitive social structures can reveal differences in perspectives on reciprocity between actors [49]. For example, Actor A perceives Actor B as a strong tie, whereas Actor B reports Actor A as a weak tie. Comparing the perspectives generated by each actor provides clues to the structure of the overall network. With this tool, Krackhardt [50] studied the flow of managerial advice in a manufacturing organization. He asked each of 21 managers to report which other managers they would contact for advice. Using both in-degree (number of nominations by other managers for actor n) and out-degree (number of nominations by actor n of other managers) information, Krackhardt examined whether managers' perceptions matched actual preferences for soliciting advice. Managers who had more accurate perceptions were rated as more powerful by others in the network, and neither formal position nor being more central improved managers' accuracy.

4.2.3. Content of ties

Researchers can explore the quantity, quality, and type of content within directed relationships. Fourth, building on the content of exchanges by combining directionality with distance, investigators can assess the relative value of exchanges among indirect ties. For example, consider a network in which Actors A–B–C are linked in sequence, where A–C is an indirect tie and A–B and B–C are direct ties. If the gradient between B and C is towards B, A would find it more difficult to access C through B. Thus, even though it would first appear that B is in a position to benefit as an entrepreneurial broker, A might be better off simply expanding the additional resources needed to contact C directly.

Collecting directional network information increases the complexity of research designs. Network analysts have addressed this problem by using a single case approach, such as Krackhardt's [50] study in a small high-tech firm, or by selecting a predefined entity with subgroups and collecting detailed information on their members, such as Klein et al.'s [47] study of teams in a service-learning program. Although the latter approach sacrifices network size for greater depth of content (based on subgroup size), other benefits follow. For example, researchers can conduct multi-level analyses by comparing network configurations within and across subgroups.

Although researchers obtaining directional network data in entrepreneurial settings confront significant data collection hurdles, they can sometimes overcome obstacles by making simplifying assumptions. For example, if collecting full network data on entrepreneurs within a defined boundary is problematic, a researcher can construct ego-network data by relying one ego's report of alters, as shown in several studies. Ruef, Aldrich, and Carter [75] studied entrepreneurial start-up teams and found that most entrepreneurs worked alone or with one other person, most likely a spouse. A related study found that entrepreneurs contacted only a few other individuals for advice, with most advisors being family members [46]. In these studies, researchers sacrificed global network coverage by using ego-network data rather than trying to survey the alters named by ego. In cases where collecting global network data is out of the question, collecting data from individuals may be the only option.

4.3. Network prestige

In Friendster, users can post testimonials for their network partners. Based on this information, other users can initiate a new relationship. Users with consistently positive endorsements across their networks will benefit by attracting more potential network partners. In an entrepreneurial setting, prestigious actors attract potential investors (e.g., angel investors who are willing back an untested idea with financial resources) or customers (e.g., web blogs spreading positive comments on a new service). Local government officials and community organizations, such as the Chamber of Commerce, will entice a prestigious and highly visible corporation to relocate into their community with favorable tax incentives and subsidies in return for the creation of jobs and the possibility of subsequently luring other firms to their area. Trade associations hire well-connected lobbyists to pitch favorable legislation for their constituent organizational members and to create a more favorable environment for the emergence of new firms.

Using directed tie information, we can expand on the centrality measures described above to measure an actor's prestige within a network [86]. Actor prestige can be measured in four ways. First, *degree prestige* is based on the in-degree of direct ties per actor. Second, an actor's *influence domain* is based on the in-degree of both direct and indirect ties. Third, an actor's *proximity prestige* reflects the average distance of all actors in the network to actor n, accounting for directionality. Fourth, an actor's *rank prestige* reflects each actor's degree and proximity prestige. For example, actor n's high rank prestige suggests that only a few other highly prestigious actors surround actor n in the actor's influence domain.

Without data over time, analysts will encounter endogeneity issues as they seek causal mechanisms leading certain actors to become more centrally active than others [38]. With longitudinal data, investigators can make better inferences about why some actors achieve centralized network positions and why others do not. Based on Stinchcombe's [80] imprinting thesis, we would expect that once actors achieve a centralized network position they will retain their position over time. As highly visible actors in the network, central actors will serve as role models for new actors. By imitating these models, new firms benefit from the lessons already learned by incumbent firms. Marquis [56] found evidence that new firms exhibited similar characteristics to prominent incumbent firms in local geographic regions throughout the United States.

Using centrality and prestige measures, an analyst can identify key network actors and the positions they occupy and thus predict who will take effective entrepreneurial action. In a network with low group level centrality (i.e., no single actor stands out as being a highly central figure), an entrepreneur belongs to a fragmented or disconnected network. For example, the network may be heterogeneous with dissimilar individuals who have not been able to overcome social barriers and form strong relationships. Low group level centrality can also imply that a high level of trust exists among network actors. Because most actors can be trusted to follow through on their commitments, each actor is equally important and accessible and no single actor stands out as centrally active. For example, Lazerson and Lorenzoni noted that in many Italian industrial districts high levels of trust allowed firms to achieve effective collective action without central actors controlling the network.

If a group has several prestigious actors, actors in the network may become reliant on them, especially in the short-term. New businesses may look to prestigious actors for financial resources or to establish legitimacy [82]. Without other options to obtain necessary resources, entrepreneurs with limited influence domain and network reach will become vulnerable to opportunistic behavior by the prestigious actors. In the Prato district, large mills, such as European Wool and the Best Group, can force their subcontractors to switch product lines or undertake significant capital investments in return for future business. These larger mills can also extend preferential transaction terms to incumbent subcontractors over new firms. To survive and grow, new firms in the district need to overcome the barriers established by the few centrally active mills.

4.4. Summary

We began this Section concerning why and how some actors are more central than others by noting the difference between taking a participant's versus an analyst's view. We noted that if entrepreneurs operate only with locally biased knowledge, their actions are blind. Although they may intuitively grasp the value of certain strategic actions, their actions are constrained by network configurations affecting their centrality, directional ties, and prestige. However, given limited knowledge, there are some possible scenarios for strategically minded entrepreneurs. First, they should move towards network positions that increase rank prestige by increasing the size of their influence domain. This requires developing additional in-degrees of direct and indirect ties. Increasing rank prestige may occur by moving closer to other prestigious actors [27]. To do this, entrepreneurs may need to change the composition of organizational affiliations, dropping less prestigious relationships in favor of more prestigious ones. Aside from building relationships with prestigious actors, an entrepreneur can work at cultivating a personal network to become more centrally active.

5

Summary and conclusions

Social capital refers to the social connections people use to obtain resources they would otherwise acquire through expending their human or financial capital. Although the study of social networks has attracted anthropologists and sociologists for over half a century, their instrumental value in modern commercial life only gained recognition within the past few decades. As entrepreneurs became preoccupied with "networking" in the 1980s, entrepreneurship and strategy researchers turned to the literature on social networks for guidance in studying the phenomenon. Many treatments were pragmatic and optimistic, with popular media often portraying networking as the key to entrepreneurial success.

We offered the example displayed in Figure 1.1 as an antidote to the superficial claim that social networks and the social capital embedded therein were an avenue to easy success. Instead, we noted that three socio-cultural constraints limit access to social capital. First, individuals with similar backgrounds and interests tend to associate with one another, rather than with people having dissimilar backgrounds, thus generating social networks characterized by low diversity. Indeed, networks are often homogenous along key dimensions, such as race, age, and sex. Second, people live within the boundaries of family and kinship relations and other semi-permeable communities. Strong boundaries deflect social relationships back upon themselves, creating and maintaining concentrated social networks. Third, because individuals lack clairvoyance and thus cannot know the full potential of pursuing indirect network ties, ignorance and uncertainty limit their activities. People often ignore potentially valuable relationships and unknowingly cultivate ties that harm them.

Thus, despite the great promise of earning high returns on their social capital, social realities often compromise that dream. Whereas entrepreneurs' social ties potentially link them to dissimilar others located within their communities, the three socio-cultural constraints we have noted complicate completely instrumental action. We thus need to investigate more thoroughly the social and cultural context of entrepreneurial networking. We have argued that concepts from social network theory give us the tools to understand the association between social capital and entrepreneurship.

In this Section, we presented social network concepts and principles via an examination of three broad empirical observations: (1) Relationships tend towards homogeneity; (2) Relationships vary in strength and distance; and (3) Individuals seek certain actors more than others. Homogeneity emerges naturally in locally dense networks. On the negative side, when locally homogeneous networks are not connected to one another, entrepreneurs face limited access to new resources and knowledge. On the positive side, network closure creates benefits for entrepreneurs because people share similar knowledge and feel secure. We argued that the benefits of social capital fall mainly to entrepreneurs able to develop a broader, more diverse network. Otherwise, rather than pursue potential gains from a more diverse network, people working under conditions of bounded rationality tend to rely on familiar routines and settle into homogeneous relationships.

Tie strength and length affect how resources and information flow between individuals. In relationships marked by frequent interactions, emotional investment, or reciprocity, both parties enjoy opportunities to discuss business matters and exchange relevant information. Entrepreneurs embedded in strong, close ties can count on reliable knowledge and people keeping their promises. Weak, distant ties, however, often carry value via the access they provide to new information or resources. We argued that successful entrepreneurs could avoid network closure by cultivating and maintaining indirect and weak ties, building a hybrid portfolio of ties varying in strength.

Some actors are more important than others because of their centrality, the directionality of the ties in which they are involved, and their prestige. However, what seems obvious from an analyst's viewpoint may be completely incomprehensible to network participants. Nonetheless, we noted several strategic implications of our analysis. We would expect effective entrepreneurs among those most active in seeking central network positions that increase their prestige, perhaps by developing additional in-degrees of direct and indirect ties. Effective action may also entail moving closer to other prestigious actors, leaving less prestigious social locations and migrating to ones that are more prestigious.

Our discussion of key network concepts and principles has explicitly assumed an omniscient observer, positioned to see all actors and their inter-relationships. We noted that network level assessments require extensive information and adequate analytical tools to assemble information for analysis. Whereas a network analyst can make predictions about how a network might evolve over time, based on historical information, an entrepreneur cannot see into the future and is hampered by bounded rationality.

Clearly, entrepreneurs are poorly placed to conduct the types of analyses we have recommended to entrepreneurship researchers. First, individuals fall short in maximizing potential gains from their social networks because of their propensity to associate with similar people and their difficulties in managing diverse networks. Second, studying variations in relationships, such as tie strength and indirect ties, requires extensive network information. Third, even if such information could be collected, strategically-minded entrepreneurs wishing to apply lessons learned by network analysts will have to find centrally active actors. In practice, many of the conclusions derived by analysts will be difficult to implement.

Friendster began in 2002 amidst great optimism about using technology to facilitate social networking and leverage someone's social capital. Other web sites emerged to ride the surging social network wave. By 2005, investors were anxious, many executives had left, users were defecting to other websites, and yet Friendster was still promising great things to come. Despite proponents' initial enthusiasm for automating the networking process, its full promise has yet to be realized. Friendster's creators placed their faith in the power of technology, but perhaps their faith was misplaced. In the final analysis, barriers of homophily, social boundaries, and bounded rationality still prevent entrepreneurs from straightforwardly achieving the optimal network positions that network analysts so blithely prescribe.

References

[1] Paul S. Adler and Seok-Woo Kwon, "Social capital: prospects for a new concept," *Academy of Management Review*, vol. 27, pp. 17, 2002.

[2] Howard E. Aldrich, *Organizations and Environments*, Prentice-Hall, Englewood Cliffs, N.J., 1979.

[3] Howard E. Aldrich and David A. Whetten, "Organization sets, action sets, and networks: Making the most of simplicity," In: *Handbook of Organizational Design*, Nystrom, P. and Starbuck, W. H., Oxford University Press, New York, pp. 385–408, 1981.

[4] Howard E. Aldrich and Nancy M. Carter, "Social networks," In: *Handbook of Entrepreneurial Dynamics: The Process of Business Creation in Contemporary America*, Gartner, W. B., Shaver, K. G., Carter, N. M., and Reynolds, P. D., Sage, Thousand Oaks, CA, 2004.

[5] John C. Almack, "The influence of intelligence on the selection of associates," *School and Society*, vol. 16, pp. 529–530, 1922.

[6] Arrow, Holly, Joseph Edward McGrath, and Jennifer L. Berdahl, *Small groups as complex systems: Formation, coordination, development and adaptation*, Sage Publications, Thousand Oaks, CA, 2000.

[7] Wayne E. Baker, "Market networks and corporate behavior," *American Journal of Sociology*, vol. 96, pp. 589, 1990.

[8] Wayne E. Baker, *Achieving Success Through Social Capital: Tapping the Hidden Resources in Your Personal and Business Networks*, Jossey-Bass, San Francisco, 2000.

[9] E. Digby Baltzell, *The protestant establishment: Aristocracy & caste in America*, Random House, New York, 1964.

[10] Nicole W. Biggart, "Banking on each other: The situational logic of rotating savings and credit associations," In: *Advances in Qualitative Organization Research*, Wagner, J. A., Bartunek, J. M., and Elsbach, K. D., JAI Press, Greenwich, CT, vol. 3, pp. 129–153, 2001.

[11] Peter M. Blau, "A macrosociological theory of social structure," *American Journal of Sociology*, vol. 83, pp. 26–54, 1977.

[12] Jeremy Boissevain, *Friends of Friends: Networks, Manipulators and Coalitions*, St. Martin's Press, New York, 1974.

[13] Helen Bott, "Observation of play activities in a nursery school," *Genetic Psychology Monographs*, vol. 4, pp. 44–88, 1928.

[14] Daniel J. Brass, Kenneth D. Butterfield, and Bruce C. Skaggs, "Relationships and unethical behavior: A social network perspective," *Academy of Management Review*, vol. 23, pp. 14–31, 1998.

[15] Ronald L. Breiger, "The duality of persons and groups," *Social Forces*, vol. 53, pp. 181–190, 1974.

[16] Ronald S. Burt, *Social Structure of Competition*, Harvard University Press, 1992.

[17] Ronald S. Burt, "A note on social capital and network context," *Social Networks*, vol. 19, pp. 355–373, 1997.

[18] Ronald S. Burt, "The network structure of social capital," In: *Research in Organizational Behavior*, Sutton, R. I. and Staw, B. M., JAI Press, Greenwich, CT, vol. 22, pp. 345–423, 2000.

[19] Kathleen Carley, "A theory of group stability," *American Sociological Review*, vol. 56, pp. 331, 1991.

[20] James S. Coleman, "Social capital in the creation of human capital," *The American Journal of Sociology*, vol. 94, pp. S95, 1988.

[21] Benjamin Cornwell and Jill Ann Harrison, "Union members and voluntary associations: Membership overlap as a case of organizational embeddedness," *American Sociological Review*, vol. 69, pp. 862, 2004.

[22] Amy E. Davis, Linda A. Renzulli, and Howard E. Aldrich, "Mixing or matching?: The influence of voluntary associations on the occupational diversity and density of small business owners' networks," *Work and Occupations*, Forthcoming.

[23] Gerald F. Davis and Henrich R. Greve, "Corporate elite networks and governance changes in the 1980s," *American Journal of Sociology*, vol. 103, pp. 1, 1997.

[24] William Domhoff, G., *The Bohemian Grove and Other Retreats: A Study in Ruling-Class Cohesiveness*, Harper & Row, New York, 1974.

[25] Michael O. Emerson and Christian Smith, *Divided by Faith: Evangelical Religion and the Problem of Race in America*, Oxford University Press, Oxford; New York, 2000.

[26] J. A. English-Lueck, *Cultures@Silicon Valley*, Stanford University Press, Stanford, Calif., 2002.

[27] Scott L. Feld, "Why your friends have more friends than you do," *American Journal of Sociology*, vol. 96, pp. 1464, 1991.

[28] Roberto M. Fernandez, Emilio J. Castilla, and Paul Moore, "Social capital at work: Networks and employment at a phone center," *American Journal of Sociology*, vol. 105, pp. 1288–1356, 2000.

[29] Ben Fine, *Social Capital versus Social Theory: Political Economy and Social Science at the Turn of the Millennium*, Routledge, London; New York, 2001.

[30] Claude S. Fischer, *To Dwell Among Friends: Personal Networks in Town and City*, University of Chicago Press, Chicago, 1982.

[31] Noah E. Friedkin, "Structural cohesion and equivalence explanations of social homogenity," *Sociological Methods and Research*, vol. 12, pp. 235–61, 1984.

[32] Joseph Galaskiewicz, *Social Organization of an Urban Grants Economy: A Study of Business Philanthropy and Nonprofit Organizations*, Academic Press, Orlando, 1985.

[33] Gargiulo, Martin, and Mario Benassi, "Trapped in your own net? Network cohesion, structural holes, and the adaptation of social capital," *Organization Science*, vol. 11, pp. 183–196, 2000.

[34] Jennifer Glanville, "Voluntary associations and social network structure: The importance of organization type," *Sociological Forum*, vol. 19, pp. 465–491, 2004.

[35] Roger V. Gould, "Collective action and network structure," *American Sociological Review*, vol. 58, pp. 182–196, 1993.

[36] Mark Granovetter, "Economic action and social structure: The problem of embeddedness," *American Journal of Sociology*, vol. 91, pp. 481–510, 1985.

[37] Mark S. Granovetter, "The strength of weak ties," *American Journal of Sociology*, vol. 78, pp. 1360–1380, 1973.

[38] Gulati, Ranjay, and Martin Gargiulo, "Where do interorganizational networks come from?," *American Journal of Sociology*, vol. 104, pp. 1439–1493, 1999.

[39] M. T. Hansen, "The search-transfer problem: The role of weak ties in sharing knowledge across organization subunits," *Administrative Science Quarterly*, vol. 44, pp. 82–111, 1999.

[40] Homans and George Caspar, *The Human Group*, Harcourt Brace, New York, 1950.

[41] Michael Hout, "Status, autonomy, and training in occupational mobility," *American Journal of Sociology*, vol. 89, pp. 1379–1409, 1984.

[42] Jeanne S. Hurlbert, Valerie A. Haines, and John J. Beggs, "Core networks and tie activation: What kinds of routine networks allocate resources in nonroutine situations?," *American Sociological Review*, vol. 65, pp. 598–618, 2000.

[43] Herminia Ibarra, "Race, opportunity, and diversity of social circles in managerial networks," *Academy of Management Journal*, vol. 38, pp. 673, 1995.

[44] Charles Kadushin, "Too much investment in social capital?," *Social Networks*, vol. 26, pp. 75–90, 2004.

[45] Rosabeth Moss Kanter, *Men and Women of the Corporation*, Basic Books, New York, 1977.

[46] Phillip H. Kim, *All in the family: Advisory networks of new ventures*, Paper presented at Academy of Management meetings, Honolulu, HI, 2005.

[47] Katherine J Klein, Beng-Chong Lim, Jessica L Saltz, and David M Mayer, "How do they get there? An examination of the antecedents of centrality in team networks," *Academy of Management Journal*, vol. 47, pp. 952, 2004.

[48] Frank H. Knight, *Risk, Uncertainty and Profit*, Houghton Mifflin Company, Boston, New York, 1921.

[49] David Krackhardt, "Cognitive social structures," *Social Networks*, vol. 9, pp. 109–134, 1987.

[50] David Krackhardt, "Assessing the political landscape: Structure, cognition, and power in organizations," *Administrative Science Quarterly*, vol. 35, pp. 342–369, 1990.

[51] Paul Lazarsfeld and Robert K. Merton, "Friendship as a social process: A substantive and methodological analysis," In: *Freedom and Control in Modern Society*, Berger, M., Abel, T., and Page, C., Octagon Books, New York, pp. 18–66, 1954.

[52] Mark H. Lazerson and Gianni Lorenzoni, "The firms that feed industrial districts: A return to the Italian source," *Industrial and Corporate Change*, vol. 8, pp. 235, 1999.

[53] Nan Lin, *Social Capital: A Theory of Social Structure and Action*, Cambridge University Press, Cambridge, UK, 2001.

[54] James G. March and Herbert A. Simon, *Organizations*, Wiley, New York, 1958.

[55] Noah Mark, "Birds of a feather sing together," *Social Forces*, vol. 77, pp. 453–485, 1998.

[56] Christopher Marquis, "The pressure of the past: Network imprinting in intercorporate communities," *Administrative Science Quarterly*, vol. 48, pp. 655–689, 2003.

[57] Peter V. Marsden, "Core discussion networks of Americans," *American Sociological Review*, vol. 52, pp. 122, 1987.

[58] Peter V. Marsden and Karen E. Campbell, "Measuring tie strength," *Social Forces*, vol. 63, pp. 482–501, 1984.

[59] J Miller McPherson and Lynn Smith-Lovin, "Sex segregation in voluntary associations," *American Sociological Review*, vol. 51, pp. 61, 1986.

[60] J Miller McPherson and Lynn Smith-Lovin, "Homophily in voluntary organizations: Status distance and the composition of face-to-face groups," *American Sociological Review*, vol. 52, pp. 370, 1987.

[61] Miller McPherson, "An ecology of affiliation," *American Sociological Review*, vol. 48, pp. 519–532, 1983.

[62] Miller McPherson, Lynn Smith-Lovin, and James M Cook, "Birds of a feather: Homophily in social networks," *Annual Review of Sociology*, vol. 27, pp. 415, 2001.

[63] Stanley Milgram, "The small world problem," *Psychology Today*, vol. 2, pp. 60–67, 1967.

[64] Janine Nahapiet and Sumantra Ghoshal, "Social capital, intellectual capital, and the organizational advantage," *Academy of Management Review*, vol. 23, pp. 242–266, 1998.

[65] Andrea R. Nierenberg, *Nonstop networking: How to improve your life, luck, and career*, Capital Books, Sterling, Va., 2002.

[66] Yusheng Peng, "Kinship networks and entrepreneurs in China's transitional economy," *American Journal of Sociology*, vol. 109, pp. 1045, 2004.

[67] Bernice A. Pescosolido and Beth A. Rubin, "The web of group affiliations revisited: Social life, postmodernism, and sociology," *American Sociological Review*, vol. 65, pp. 52–76, 2000.

[68] Joel M. Podolny, "Networks as the pipes and prisms of the market," *The American Journal of Sociology*, vol. 107, pp. 33, 2001.

[69] Pamela A. Popielarz and J. Miller McPherson, "On the edge or in between: Niche position, niche overlap, and the duration of voluntary association memberships," *American Journal of Sociology*, vol. 101, pp. 698, 1995.

[70] Alejandro Portes, "SOCIAL CAPITAL: Its origins and applications in modern sociology," *Annual Review of Sociology*, vol. 24, pp. 1, 1998.

[71] Robert Putnam, *Bowling Alone: The Collapse and Revival of American Community*, Simon & Schuster, New York, 2000.

[72] Ray Reagans and Ezra W. Zuckerman, "Networks, diversity, and productivity: The social capital of corporate R&D teams," *Organization Science*, vol. 12, pp. 502, 2001.

[73] Linda A. Renzulli, Howard Aldrich, and James Moody, "Family matters: Gender, networks, and entrepreneurial outcomes," *Social Forces*, vol. 79, pp. 523–546, 2000.

[74] Charlie Rose, "The Charlie Rose Show," New York, 2004.

[75] Ruef, Martin, Howard E. Aldrich, and Nancy M. Carter, "The structure of founding teams: Homophily, strong ties, and isolation among U.S. entrepreneurs," *American Sociological Review*, vol. 68, pp. 195–222, 2003.

[76] AnnaLee Saxenian, *Regional Advantage: Culture and Competition in Silicon Valley and Route 128*, Harvard University Press, Cambridge, Mass., 1994.

[77] Olav Sorenson and Pino G. Audia, "The social structure of entrepreneurial activity: Geographic concentration of footwear production in the United States, 1940-1989," *American Journal of Sociology*, vol. 106, pp. 424, 2000.

[78] Udo Staber, "Sociology and economic development policy: The case of industrial district promotion," *Canadian Journal of Sociology*, vol. 23, pp. 239, 1998.

[79] Alex Stewart, *Team Entrepreneurship*, Sage Publications, Newbury Park, 1989.

[80] Arthur Stinchcombe, "Organizations and social structure," In: *Handbook of Organizations*, March, J. G., Rand McNally, Chicago, pp. 142–193, 1965.

[81] David Strang and Nancy Brandon Tuma, "Spatial and temporal heterogeneity in diffusion," *American Journal of Sociology*, vol. 99, pp. 614, 1993.

[82] Toby E. Stuart, Ha Hoang, and Ralph C. Hybels, "Interorganizational endorsements and the performance of entrepreneurial ventures," *Administrative Science Quarterly*, vol. 44, pp. 315–349, 1999.

[83] Toby E. Stuart and Olav Sorenson, "Liquidity events and the geographic distribution of entrepreneurial activity," *Administrative Science Quarterly*, vol. 48, pp. 175–201, 2003.

[84] Michael Useem, *The inner Circle: Large Corporations and the Rise of Business Political Activity in the U.S. and U.K*, Oxford University Press, New York, 1984.

[85] Brian Uzzi, "The sources and consequences of embeddedness for the economic performance of organizations: The network effect," *American Sociological Review*, vol. 61, pp. 674, 1996.

[86] Stanley Wasserman and Katherine Faust, *Social Network Analysis: Methods and Applications*, Cambridge University Press, Cambridge, 1994.

[87] Duncan J. Watts, *Six Degrees: The Science of a Connected Age*, Norton, New York, 2003.

[88] Beth Wellman, "The school child's choice of companions," *Journal of Educational Research*, vol. 14, pp. 126–132, 1926.

[89] Oliver E. Williamson, "The economics of organization: The transaction cost approach," *American Journal of Sociology*, vol. 87, pp. 548–577, 1981.

Foundations and Trends™ in
Technology, Information and Operations Management
Vol 1, No 1 (2005) 1-58

the essence of knowledge

Social Capital and Entrepreneurship

Phillip H. Kim and Howard E. Aldrich

Abstract

We offer a critical review of the concepts and principles of social capital
and social networks as applied to entrepreneurship. Our review is
intended for junior scholars and graduate students in the field of
entrepreneurship who wish to learn the basic vocabulary of social network
and social capital analyses. We illustrate several interesting
research questions and a toolbox of methods to answer them. First, we
use a popular new website, Friendster, to show the potential power of
social capital accessed via social networks. Then, we show that the
potential of social networks often cannot be realized because of various
socio-cultural constraints. Taking account of these constraints, we offer
three empirical generalizations about social networks and show how
the concepts of homophily, social boundaries, and bounded rationality
provide a framework for understanding the observations. As we discuss
each generalization, we discuss some well-established theoretical contri-
butions and empirical findings from the social capital and social networks literatures. Throughout the text we explain various research
designs for studying social networks and issues raised in trying to use
them. We conclude by noting the tension between the properties of
social networks used in entrepreneurship researchers' models and the
limited perspective on networks available to practicing entrepreneurs.